Mother Teresa

REV. JUDE WINKLER, OF

Imprimi Potest: **Michael Kolodziej, OFM Conv.**, Minister Provincial of St. Anthony of Padua Province (USA)
Nihil Obstat: **Sr. Kathleen Flanagan, S.C., Ph.D.**, Censor Librorum
Imprimatur: ✠ **Frank J. Rodimer, J.C.D.**, Bishop of Paterson

The Nihil Obstat and Imprimatur are official declarations that a book or pamphlet is free of doctrinal or moral error. No implication is contained therein that those who have granted the Nihil Obstat and Imprimatur agree with the contents, opinions or statements expressed.

© 2002 by CATHOLIC BOOK PUBLISHING CORP., Totowa, N.J.
Printed in Hong Kong   ISBN 978-0-89942-519-1

MOTHER TERESA'S CHILDHOOD

MOTHER Teresa was born on August 26, 1910, in the city of Skopje. Her family was Albanian, but their city is now a part of Macedonia. She was baptized the next day and given the name Agnes. Even though most people who are Albanian are Muslims, the members of Agnes' family were fervent Catholics. Agnes' parents, Nikola and Dranafile, were loving parents and dedicated to their faith.

Agnes' family was quite well off. Her father was a merchant who was intelligent and who traveled a great deal. He died when Agnes was only eight years old. This was a terrible loss for Agnes and her mother, as well as for her brother Lazar and her sister Aga.

The family lost much of their wealth. Agnes' mother worked hard to provide for her family and taught her about charity toward those who had even less. There were frequent guests at their table. Agnes' mother often took her on trips to bring food to those who were very poor.

Agnes learned that one must love and serve those less fortunate than oneself—in accord with her father's words: "My child, never eat a single mouthful unless you are sharing it with others."

MOTHER TERESA'S CALLING

AGNES continued to learn about her faith from her mother and from her parish. The pastor at Sacred Heart church worked with the children of her city to teach them and to organize church activities. He also shared many stories with them about the activities of the Jesuit missionaries who had opened a mission in Calcutta, India.

Agnes began to think about joining the convent when she was twelve years old. Over the next six years her vocation matured, and she spoke to her mother about becoming a sister.

At first, Agnes' mother said no, but Agnes continued to speak to her about her call. Agnes' mother was not really opposed to her daughter's vocation. She only wanted to make sure that Agnes was convinced about her decision. When she finally gave her daughter permission, she told her that she must live, "only, all for God and Jesus."

Agnes had originally thought of going to Africa, but the stories she had heard about India led her to the Sisters of Loretto, a community that served in Calcutta. On September 26 of 1928, she left home to travel to the sisters' motherhouse in Dublin, Ireland.

AGNES spent six weeks in Dublin where she began instruction in English, the language that she would use for the rest of her life. Then on December 1, she and another companion boarded a ship for India. It was at this time that she took the name Sister Mary Teresa of the Child Jesus. She wanted to be like St. Therese who sought to please God by doing simple things with great love.

Sister Teresa arrived in India on January 6, 1929, and began her two year novitiate (two years of prayer and study) on May 23. She continued to perfect her English, and also studied two of the major languages of India: Hindi and Bengali. Fortunately, she was very good at languages.

Sister Teresa made her first, temporary vows on May 24, 1931. She began teaching in the schools of the Sisters of Loretto. Even while she was teaching, though, she spent some time nursing. She was moved by the horrible poverty of the people. On Sundays she would visit the slums of Calcutta where the poorest of the poor lived.

On May 24, 1937, she professed the vows of poverty, chastity, and obedience for the rest of her life.

MOTHER TERESA'S INSPIRATION

S omething was going on in Sister Teresa's heart. She prayed and spoke to her spiritual director, Father Celeste Van Exem.

Then in September of 1946 her superiors sent Sister Teresa out of the city to a house in the mountains so that she could recover her health. She had always been a bit unhealthy, and lately she had grown weaker and weaker.

On September 10, Sister Teresa boarded the train. It was there that she had her inspiration to leave the Sisters of Loretto and to found a new community of sisters. They would not wait for the poor to come to them—they would go out to the poor.

Sister Teresa realized that this would be very difficult work, but it would be based upon a profound life of prayer. It is this relationship with the Lord that would lead the sisters to serve the poor and give them the strength to do it.

Sister Teresa was especially inspired by three scenes from the Bible. The first was when Jesus said that He thirsted on the Cross. She felt that He thirsted for souls and that we should serve those who thirsted or were hungry.

MOTHER TERESA SEEKS PERMISSION

THE second Bible scene that inspired Sister Teresa was when Jesus met the Samaritan woman at the well. He asked her to give Him a drink. Likewise, He asks us to provide for those who are in need.

Finally, there was the scene of the Visitation of Mary to her cousin Elizabeth. Mary went in haste to help Elizabeth. We, too, should also go in haste to help the poor.

Sister Teresa told her inspiration to her spiritual director. He and she prayed upon this call for the next several months.

They then went to the Archbishop. He was very hesitant, and asked her to wait for at least a year. After quite some time he approved of her request to write to Rome and ask for permission to begin her new community.

It was only in April of 1948 that she received her letter of permission to leave the Sisters of Loretto for one year to try her experiment. It was not until August 16 of that year that all was ready and Sister Teresa exchanged her habit as a Sister of Loretto for her new habit, a white sari lined in blue.

THE FIRST MISSIONARY SISTERS OF CHARITY

OVER the next few months, Mother Teresa received some training in medicine. Then, that December, she began her work in the slums of Calcutta. She opened a school for small children and a home for sick and dying people.

Mother Teresa moved into her new home in February of 1949, and on March 19 her first disciple arrived. Sister Agnes had been one of Mother Teresa's students and she felt an intense devotion to her. By the end of April her second disciple had arrived, and the next month there was a third. Within a short time Mother Teresa had eleven disciples.

It was now time to receive official permission to found a new congregation of sisters. Father Van Exem and her Archbishop sent the request to Rome along with a description of what Mother had already accomplished. Mother was given approval by Pope Pius XII on October 7, 1950, the Feast of the Holy Rosary. In April of 1953, the first of Mother Teresa's followers made their temporary vows as Missionary Sisters of Charity.

14

THE HOUSE FOR THE DYING

THE sisters live a very simple life-style. They depend upon the generosity of their benefactors. They often have no idea of where their next meal will come from, but they trust in God's love and mercy. They perform the most humbling of services for those who are in need.

Mother Teresa trained her sisters so that they could be of service to the poor. Some were even trained as doctors, something unusual for women in India in those days.

One of the sisters' earliest works was to provide a loving home for those who were dying. Calcutta was so poor that people often died along the side of the streets. The sisters brought those who were dying to their home. There they were cleaned, fed, and treated. Most of all they were loved. They would not have to die alone and frightened.

The sisters took in Christians, Hindus, and Muslims. At first some feared that the sisters were only doing this to convert the dying. Yet, as people saw the love with which the sisters treated the dying, they were won over and even became benefactors of the sisters.

MOTHER Teresa and the sisters began working with orphans and abandoned children. The sisters took them in and fed them and taught them a skill so that they could earn a living.

They also began to work among those who suffered from leprosy. Lepers were often abandoned by their families. One person told Mother Teresa that he would not work with or even touch a leper for a thousand pounds (the money used in England). Mother Teresa responded that neither would she. The only thing that would get her to help a leper is the love of God.

Mother Teresa also established ambulances that could travel to where the lepers lived. This way, they would be able to serve many more people than if all the lepers were to come and live at their centers. She also founded villages where leper families could live with dignity and work for a living.

Mother Teresa always insisted that the sisters not use gloves when they treated the lepers. Those who had leprosy needed to experience the love of people who were not afraid to touch them.

THE MISSION SPREADS

THE community continued to grow. Church law decreed that a new community could not spread beyond its diocese for the first ten years. Yet, the need in India was so great that the first convents in other dioceses were established in 1959, a year before the ten-year period had ended. In 1965, Pope Paul VI declared that the community was now under the authority of the Holy Father.

This was the same year that the sisters opened their first convents outside of India. Mother Teresa was not sure that the sisters were ready, but the cardinal who invited her told her that she should not think of the needs of the sisters as much as the needs of the Church. The sisters opened a house in Venezuela, where they aided the poor and taught children the faith.

Within the next few years, there were new houses in Tanzania, Rome, Jordan, England, and Northern Ireland. Wherever they went, the sisters lived among the poorest of the poor. They not only lived with them; they also lived like them. They often rejected gifts that would have meant that they owned more than their neighbors.

THE sisters' numbers continued to grow. Twenty years after the beginning of the community, there were already 158 foundations throughout the world with over 1,100 sisters and over 400 novices (young women who were preparing to make their vows in the community).

Yet, the great growth was not the most important thing. Mother wanted the sisters to remain faithful to their original calling. She said:

> "Believe me, Sisters, all will be well if we surrender ourselves and we obey. Obey the Church, obey the Holy Father because he loves us tenderly and he wants us really to be the spouses of Jesus crucified."

> "Our young people want holiness, that complete surrender to God."

She also said:

> "I did not know that our work would grow so fast or go so far. I never doubted that it would live, but I did not think that it would be like this. Doubt I never had, because I had this conviction that if God blesses it, it will prosper. . . . This is the miracle of all those little sisters and people all around the world. God is using them—they are just little instruments in His hands."

OTHERS ARE CALLED

THE call to serve the poorest of the poor extended beyond the original group of the Missionary Sisters of Charity. In 1963, three men came forward and asked to live this same calling. This was the beginning of the Missionary Brothers of Charity. This community grew slowly, and it was only in 1967 that they officially became a new congregation.

The goal of the brothers was:

> **"To live this life of love by dedicating oneself to the service of the poorest of the poor in slums, on the streets and wherever they are found. Leprosy patients, destitute beggars, the abandoned, homeless boys, and young men in the slums, the unemployed and those uprooted by war and disaster will always be the special object of the Brothers' concern."**

Soon there were two other branches of the Missionaries of Charity for men: a group of brothers who spend much more time in prayer called the Brothers of the World and a group of priests dedicated to serving the poorest of the poor. A new group of sisters dedicated to a life of greater prayer also developed.

THE GIFT OF SUFFERING

MOTHER Teresa saw suffering as a special calling from the Lord. She understood that there is a great spiritual value that can be found in a surrender to God's will. In 1953, she said to those who were suffering:

> "Your suffering and prayers will be the chalice in which we the working members will pour in the love of souls we gather round. Therefore, you are just as important and necessary for the fulfillment of our aim. . . . In reality you can do much more while on your bed of pain than I running on my feet, but you and I together can do all things in Him Who strengthens me."

Thus, Mother Teresa showed that there is a different way to look at life. Often those suffering become angry or depressed. Mother taught them that if they trusted in God's love they would become a great source of holiness in the world. This is why she also wrote:

> "My very dear children, let us love Jesus with our whole heart and soul. Let us bring Him many souls. Keep smiling. There is nothing special for you to do but to allow Jesus to live His life in you by accepting whatever He gives and giving whatever He takes with a big smile."

MOTHER Teresa's work and her love of God began to become famous throughout the world. Authors began to write about her teachings. They were simple words that she shared with the world, but words that touched the hearts of all who read them.

She wrote:

"Be kind and merciful. Let no one ever come to you without coming away better and happier."

"The best way to show our gratitude to God and people is to accept everything with joy."

"Prayer enlarges the heart until it is capable of containing the gift that God makes of Himself."

"Because we cannot see God, we cannot express our love to Him in person. But our neighbor we can see, and we can do for him or her what we would love to do for Jesus if He were visible."

"Joy is a net of love by which we can capture souls. God loves the person who gives with joy."

MOTHER TERESA RECEIVES
THE NOBEL PEACE PRIZE

THE world also began to recognize Mother Teresa's work by granting her various awards. In 1971, Pope Paul VI gave Mother Teresa the Pope John XXIII Peace Prize. Mother accepted this prize and used the money to help build a center for lepers in India. The next year she was given the Nehru Award by the Indian government in recognition of her works of charity throughout the world.

She has been honored by governments and universities and organizations all throughout the world. She used all of these opportunities to speak to those in power on how they should serve the poor.

Then in 1979 Mother Teresa received one of the most famous awards given in the world: The Nobel Peace Prize. It was given to her in Oslo, Norway, that December. She said:

> **"I think that this is something, that we must live life beautifully, we have Jesus with us and He loves us. If we could only remember that God loves us, and we have an opportunity to love others as He loves us, not in big things, but in small things with great love."**

MOTHER'S HEALTH FAILS

Mother Teresa continued to travel throughout the world, speaking to people about serving the poor.

She also carried the responsibility of directing the order throughout the world (which by then had grown to thousands of sisters). In 1990, she tried to resign as Mother General, but the sisters insisted that she carry on. In a spirit of obedience, she continued to carry that burden.

But in 1991 her health began to show the first signs of failure. In December of that year she ended up in the hospital with heart problems. She was treated and quickly returned to health. Over the next few years she would have some periods of good health when she could travel, and then other periods when she was kept to her bed.

On September 5, 1997, Mother Teresa's heart failed and she went home to the Lord. Thousands of people, the great and the small, the powerful and the poorest of the poor, came to pay respect to this holy woman who had tried throughout her life to do something beautiful for God.

FOR THE GLORY OF GOD

MANY people believe that Mother Teresa will soon be canonized. On October 19, 2003, in fact, she was proclaimed to be Blessed, which is the last step before she is declared to be a Saint. Her simple faith and her great love for God and the poor are a source of wonder to all who knew her.

Yet, in spite of the fame she achieved, she did not become proud. She remained humble and loving and gentle. She told her sisters:

> **"I am only a small instrument in God's hand. Our Lord and our Lady gave all the glory to God the Father; like them, in a very, very small way, I want to give all the glory to God the Father."**